CW01660835

BELIEVE
and be
BAPTISED

Victor Jack

This edition published in Great Britain in 2017

British Library Cataloguing in Publication Data
A record for this book is available from the British Library
ISBN: 978-1-911272-33-5

Designed by Design Chapel www.design-chapel.com

Printed in the UK by Penny Print

10Publishing, a division of 10ofthose.com
Unit C, Tomlinson Road, Leyland, PR25 2DY, England
Email: info@10ofthose.com
Website: www.10ofthose.com

THE AIMS OF THIS BOOKLET

1

To provide a basic explanation of believers' baptism for those who are thinking of taking this step.

2

To provide parents with a straightforward explanation of baptism when they fail to understand the desires of their sons or daughters.

BELIEVE AND BE BAPTISED

The message Peter preached on the day of Pentecost shows us clearly the steps we need to take on our journey to faith in Jesus. It is an exciting journey which gets more and more rewarding the further we travel. These verses from Acts 2:22–47 will form the basis for most of the teaching that follows.

Men of Israel, listen to this: Jesus of Nazareth was a man accredited by God to you by miracles, wonders and signs, which God did among you through him, as you yourselves know. This man was handed over to you by God's set purpose and foreknowledge; and you, with the help of wicked men, put him to death by nailing him to the cross. But God raised him from the dead, freeing him from the agony of death, because it was impossible for death to keep its hold on him…

Therefore let all Israel be assured of this: God has made this Jesus, whom you crucified, both Lord and Christ. When the people heard this, they were cut to the heart and said to Peter and the other apostles, 'Brothers, what shall we do?'

Peter replied, 'Repent and be baptised, every one of you, in the name of Jesus Christ for the forgiveness of your sins. And you will receive the gift of the Holy Spirit. The promise is for you and your children and for all who are far off – for all whom the Lord our God will call.'

With many other words he warned them; and he pleaded with them, 'Save yourselves from this corrupt generation.' Those who accepted his message were baptised, and about three

'They broke bread in their homes and ate together with glad and sincere hearts, praising God and enjoying the favour of all the people.'

thousand were added to their number that day.

They devoted themselves to the apostles' teaching and to the fellowship, to the breaking of bread and to prayer. Everyone was filled with awe, and many wonders and miraculous signs were done by the apostles. All the believers were together and had everything in common. Selling their possessions and goods, they gave to anyone as he had need. Every day they continued to meet together in the temple courts. They broke bread in their homes and ate together with glad and sincere hearts, praising God and enjoying the favour of all the people. And the Lord added to their number daily those who were being saved. (Acts 2:22–47)

Many different pictures have been used in the Bible to illustrate what it means both to become a Christian and then to live the Christian life, such as a walk, a race and a fight. In this booklet, we shall use the picture of crossing a river by means of stepping-stones, in order to emphasise how easy it is, after setting out as a Christian, to get marooned mid-stream and then to make no further progress. God's blessing and our spiritual progress are forfeited. Just as it takes effort and courage at times to leap from one stone to another, so there are many challenging steps to take if we are to keep moving forward as Christians. One of these is baptism, which requires that we publicly declare our allegiance to Jesus. Baptism is the main subject of this booklet because too many get stranded here.

Before considering the importance of baptism, we will first trace the steps that lead up to it. This will help to make sure that we are ready to be baptised.

Step 1

CONFRONTED WITH THE TRUTH

In his message Peter confronted the people with the truth about Jesus and themselves.

THE TRUTH ABOUT JESUS

His life – Jesus was more than a man; He was the Son of God, the promised Messiah. Peter declared, *'Jesus of Nazareth was a man accredited by God to you by miracles, wonders and signs, which God did among you through him, as you yourselves knew'* (v. 22).

His Death – This was no accident but part of God's plan for our salvation. *'This man was handed over to you by God's set purpose and foreknowledge; and you, with the help of wicked men, put him to death by nailing him to the cross'* (v. 23).

His Resurrection – Men crucified Him *'but God raised him from the dead, freeing him from the agony of death, because it was impossible for death to keep its hold on him'* (v.24). The Prince of Life conquered the Prince of Death. Unlike other great leaders of the past, Jesus is alive today.

His Exaltation – Jesus was *'exalted to the right hand of God'* (v. 33) and waits for the time when God's promise will be fulfilled; *'Sit at my right hand until I* *make your enemies a footstool for your feet'* (vv. 34–35). The time is coming when He will rule the world in peace and righteousness, and everyone will know that He is Lord, to the glory of God the Father.

A fuller picture of who Jesus is can be found in two wonderful passages in the New Testament. Read and meditate on Philippians 2:5–11 and Colossians 1:15–23.

THE TRUTH ABOUT THEMSELVES

They were sinners, guilty of the death of Jesus Christ (vv. 23–36). We too are guilty, for we are part of the sinful human race for whom Jesus Christ died. God's verdict on us all is unmistakably clear: *'There is no-one righteous, not even one; there is no-one who understands, no-one who seeks God. All have turned away, they have together become worthless; there is no-one who does good, not even one'* (Romans 3:10–12).

In our hearts we know the Bible is right when it states, *'for all have sinned and fall short of the glory of God'* (Romans 3:23). We haven't lived up to our own standards or the standards God has set for us.

They must repent in order to be forgiven and receive the gift of the Holy Spirit. So must we. *'Repent and be baptised, everyone of you, in the name of Jesus Christ for the forgiveness of your sins. And you will receive the gift of the Holy Spirit'* (v. 38). Jesus taught *'unless you repent, you too will all perish'* (Luke 13:3–5). Paul declared, *'God commands all people everywhere to repent. For he has set a day when he will judge the world with justice by the man he has appointed'* (Acts 17: 30–31).

They must call on the name of the Lord for salvation, *'Lord, save me'* must be the cry of our hearts. *'And everyone who calls on the name of the Lord will be saved'* (v. 21).

They must be baptised, *'Repent and be baptised, everyone of you, in the name of Jesus Christ'* (v. 38). We too are baptised in order to show that our past has been forgiven and that we have begun to live a new life for the glory of God.

Step 2

CONVICTED BY THE TRUTH

In the next paragraph we discover how the crowd reacted to Peter's message. *'When the people heard this, they were cut to the heart'* (v. 37). Peter's message went to their consciences like an arrow to its mark. The people understood what they heard, their consciences were awakened and they knew they were guilty. The Spirit of God drove the word of God home into the hearts of the hearers in a supernatural way.

Conviction of sin is like an alarm clock, which rings and rings in our conscience until we rise from our sinful state and respond to God. We may try to silence this inner voice in our hearts, but we shall not know God's forgiveness and peace until we obey the message His Holy Spirit has impressed on our hearts.

Step 3

CONCERNED ABOUT THE TRUTH

Peter's listeners cried out, *'Brothers, what shall we do?'* (v. 37) The truth they heard enlightened their minds, awakened their consciences and now challenged their hearts. Their cry is full of anxious enquiry. To whom could they turn? How could they quieten their troubled spirits? Peter pointed them to Jesus. Those who are sick know they need to consult a doctor, and those who know they have sinned against God need to turn to Jesus, the Great Physician. Jesus said, *'It is not the healthy who need a doctor, but the sick. I have not come to call the righteous, but sinners to repentance'* (Luke 5:31–32).

Step 4

CONVERTED TO JESUS CHRIST

In answer to their question, *'What shall we do?'* Peter said, *'Repent and be baptised, every one of you in the name of Jesus Christ for the forgiveness of your sins. And you will receive the gift of the Holy Spirit.'* Those listening would know exactly what he meant, because John the Baptist had preached the necessity of repentance and then baptised those who turned to God. The people responded readily to this direct challenge. *'Those who accepted his message were baptised, and about three thousand were added to their number that day.'*

There are three pictures used in this passage to illustrate what it means to become a Christian. Each one will help us to make sure that we really belong to Jesus and are ready to be baptised in His name.

REPENTING

Repentance means to have a change of mind that leads to a change of direction in our lives.

Repentance is a basic and essential part of becoming a Christian. John the Baptist preached, *'Repent, for the kingdom of heaven is near'* (Matthew 3:1). Jesus began His ministry with the words, *'Repent, for the kingdom of heaven is near'* (Matthew 4:17). Peter declared in another sermon,

'Repent, then, and turn to God, so that your sins may be wiped out' (Acts 3:19).

We have all wandered away from God and taken the pathway in life that suited us best. We need to turn around and leave what Jesus called the *'broad road that leads to destruction'* and take the *'narrow road that leads to life'* (Matthew 7:13–14). This is repentance and it is well illustrated by the military command when marching, *'Halt, about turn, quick march.'* We need to stop and think about the life we are living. We need to do an about turn and start following the way of Jesus.

Repentance is much more than saying that we are sorry. Repentance means *'to leave the sin I loved before and show that I'm in earnest by doing so no more.'* We cannot follow Jesus without forsaking those things that we know are wrong in our lives.

CALLING

'And everyone who calls on the name of the Lord will be saved' (v. 21). Many needy people called on Jesus Christ for help during His lifetime. He heard and answered their cry.

'A man with leprosy came to him and begged him on his knees, "If you are willing, you can make me clean." Filled with compassion, Jesus reached out his hand and touched the man. "I am willing," he said. "Be clean!" Immediately the leprosy left him and he was cured' (Mark 1:40–42).

When blind Bartimaeus heard that Jesus was going down the road where he was sitting and begging *'he began to shout, "Jesus, Son of David, have mercy on me!" "Go," said Jesus, "your faith has healed you." Immediately he received his sight and followed Jesus along the road.'* (Mark 10:46–52)

If we call on Jesus in prayer, He will hear our cry and we too will be saved, which means being delivered from our sinfulness and self-centredness.

RECEIVING

In verse 41 we read that the crowd 'accepted his message' or 'received his word' (RSV). The people were willing, not only to receive God's word from Peter's lips, but also willing to receive Jesus Christ as their Lord and Master. Believing and receiving are two key words to remember when we think of becoming a Christian. We believe the truth about Jesus Christ and then we allow Him to take control of our lives. *'Yet to all who received him, to those who believed in his name, he gave the right to become children of God'* (John 1:12).

Peter also promised that those who repented would *'receive the gift of the*

Holy Spirit' (v. 38). Every person who becomes a Christian is given the precious gift of the Holy Spirit. He enables us to live the Christian life. To try and live the Christian life without the Holy Spirit is like trying to drive a car without any fuel in the tank. We will not have the power to live the way God wants us to live.

God gives us the Holy Spirit to enable us to have the inward assurance that we are His children and that He is our Father. *'The Spirit himself testifies with our spirit that we are God's children'* (Romans 8.16). *'By him we cry "Abba, Father"'* (Romans 8:15).

God gives us the Holy Spirit so that we can understand the Bible. The Holy Spirit who inspired the writing of Scripture also interprets its meaning for us. Jesus promised that the Holy Spirit will *'teach you all things and will remind you of everything I have said to you'* (John 14:26). He later added, *'When he, the Spirit of truth, comes, he will guide you into all truth'* (John 16:13).

God gives us the Holy Spirit so that we can be bold in our witness as Christians. In Acts 4:31 we read *'they were all filled with the Holy Spirit and spoke the word of God boldly.'*

Can we say that we have repented before God, trusted Jesus Christ by faith, and received the gift of the Holy Spirit? If the answer is 'Yes', then we need to be willing to obey His command to be baptised. Too many get sidetracked just here. They are converted, but do not continue to progress. Conversion is only the beginning. It is a gateway through which we pass to a completely new way of life. Having begun, we must continue and obey the command to be baptised.

If we call on Jesus in prayer, He will hear our cry and we too will be saved, which means being delivered from our sinfulness and self-centredness.

Questions to answer

1. List the important truths Peter taught the people about Jesus on the day of Pentecost.

2. Write down the two commands and the two promises Peter gave to the people in Acts 2:38.

3. Explain the meaning of repentance in your own words.

4. Outline some of the ways in which the Holy Spirit helps us in our Christian lives.

5. Give a brief account of how you became a Christian.

6. In what ways have you been helped to grow as a Christian?

Step 5

CONFESSING JESUS

'Those who accepted his message were baptised' (v. 41). Having become Christians, they were willing to show others that they belonged to Jesus. We must not remain secret disciples as though we are afraid of what others might think. We need to be bold about our faith in Jesus, and proud of our allegiance to Him. He said *'If anyone is ashamed of me and my words in this adulterous and sinful generation, the Son of Man will be ashamed of him when he comes in his Father's glory with the holy angels'* (Mark 8:38). There are three ways in which we can confess Jesus as our Lord and Master:

BY OUR LIPS

'If you confess with your mouth, "Jesus is Lord", and believe in your heart that God raised him from the dead, you will be saved. For it is with your heart that you believe and are justified, and it is with your mouth that you confess and are saved' (Romans 10:9–10).

Let us use our lips to tell our friends of Jesus and of all He has done for us. It will take courage at first, but we can go on to do this more confidently.

BY OUR LIVES

If we tell others that we are Christians, we must be careful to live like Christians, otherwise we shall be called hypocrites. *'Whatever happens, conduct yourselves in a manner worthy of the gospel of Christ'*

(Philippians 1:27). *'I urge you to live a life worthy of the calling you have received'* (Ephesians 4:1).

A changed life is always a powerful witness. People may misunderstand or misinterpret our words, but they will always notice our actions. What we do is just as important as what we say.

The witness of our lives resembles a bright light in a dark world. Jesus Christ said, *'Let your light shine before men, that they may see your good deeds and praise your Father in heaven'* (Matthew 5:16).

'Do everything without complaining or arguing, so that you may become blameless and pure, children of God without fault in a crooked and depraved generation, in which you shine like stars in the universe' (Philippians 2:14–15).

BY BEING BAPTISED

Baptism is commanded by Jesus, and is another courageous way of confessing our faith in Him. Baptism might almost be called 'The badge of discipleship'. Just as people may wear a badge to identify themselves with a certain movement, so we may look upon baptism as a way of showing people that we belong to Jesus. That is one of the reasons why we are baptised *'in the name of the Father and of the Son and of the Holy Spirit'* (Matthew 28:19). This indicates not only to whom we belong but also under whose authority we now live. Before we look at the meaning of baptism there are two points that need to be emphasised.

Baptism follows belief in Jesus

This is a simple but very important principle that is stressed again and again in the New Testament. We must be committed to Jesus before we can begin to think of confessing Jesus in baptism. A few verses from the Bible will help to impress this upon our minds. Jesus said, *'Go into all the world and preach the good news to all creation. Whoever believes and is baptised will be saved, but whoever does not believe will be condemned'* (Mark 16:15–16). *'But when they believed Philip as he preached the good news of the kingdom of God and the name of Jesus Christ, they were baptised, both men and women'.* (Acts 8:12). *'Many of the Corinthians who heard him believed and were baptised'* (Acts 18:8).

To baptise a person who has never become a true Christian is like dressing a man in uniform and declaring him to be a soldier when he has never enlisted in the army. Unless we have personally believed in Jesus, we have no faith to confess in baptism.

Baptism cannot produce salvation

Although baptism is often linked with salvation, the Bible never suggests that we can experience a spiritual change of heart by being baptised. A person is not baptised to become a Christian, but rather to show he or she is a Christian.

Anything that may be done to us outwardly cannot change us inwardly, so far as God is concerned. There are no magical powers in the water. Water can clean the hands but not the heart. In his first epistle, Peter links baptism with salvation and uses Noah's ark and the flood as an illustration. He states that baptism is *'not the removal of dirt from the body but the pledge of a good conscience towards God. It saves you by the resurrection of Jesus Christ, who has gone into heaven and is at God's right hand'* (1 Peter 3:21–22). Although the flood carried the ark to safety, Noah and his family were saved through being in the ark. We are saved through being 'in Christ', not through the waters of baptism.

Unfortunately, some think that through being baptised as children, they automatically become Christians. Their faith is in a particular religious rite, rather than in the work of Jesus Christ. Always in Scripture, salvation is by grace through faith and not by works, whether it is a good deed we perform or a rite to which we submit. *'For it is by grace you have been saved, through faith – and this not from yourselves, it is the gift of God – not by works, so that no one can boast'* (Ephesians 2:8–9).

To baptise a person who has never become a true Christian is like dressing a man in uniform and declaring him to be a soldier when he has never enlisted in the army. Unless we have personally believed in Jesus, we have no faith to confess in baptism.

BAPTISM AND ITS MEANING...

- *Why is it necessary to be baptised?*
- *What does it signify?*
- *In baptism we actively and openly make a declaration of certain facts...*

1. OUR OBEDIENCE TO JESUS CHRIST

Baptism was part of the great commission that Jesus gave to His disciples before He ascended to heaven. *‘Go and make disciples of all nations, baptising them in the name of the Father and of the Son and of the Holy Spirit, and teaching them to obey everything I have commanded you”* (Matthew 28:19–20).

They were under divine orders. As we read through the book of Acts, we see how implicitly those orders were obeyed. Every new Christian was baptised. In Acts 10:48 we discover that Peter *‘ordered that they be baptised’*, which illustrates that neither the apostles nor the new believers regarded baptism as an optional extra.

If it is the will of Jesus that every person who becomes a Christian should be baptised, then we must bow in submission to His will. We must obey

Him, not grudgingly but willingly. Before we became Christians, we thought only of pleasing ourselves, now we must make it our goal to please Him, see 2 Corinthians 5:9.

The One to whom we have given our lives is Jesus Christ the Lord. Each name is significant. Jesus is the Saviour, because He died for me. Christ is the Living One, who has come to live in me. He is Lord, which means that He is my owner, master and king. If He is my owner, I am His personal property. If He is my king I should be His loyal subject. The One who died for me, and lives in me, should rule over me.

The whole question of our obedience to Jesus is really a test of our love for Him. How willing are we to do what He wants? Jesus said, *'If you love me, you will obey what I command'* (John 14:15). Obedience that does not spring from love is a cold and clinical response.

Jesus also said, *'You are my friends if you do what I command'* (John 15:14). Nothing will foster our friendship with Jesus Christ more than willing obedience. When we discover and obey His will, this will bring an added joy to our Christian experience. Jesus said, *'Now that you know these things, you will be blessed if you do them'* (John 13: 17). *'What are you waiting for? Get up, be baptised and wash your sins away'* (Acts 22:16)

2. OUR CONFESSION OF JESUS CHRIST

Baptism has been described as 'an outward sign of an inward faith'. This is a simple but helpful definition. Faith is an invisible, intangible thing and needs to be expressed in action. We can show people what they cannot see; we can declare what they may not have already guessed, that our faith is in Jesus.

Baptism is a way of publicly showing everyone that you have faith in Jesus. A young man may become a police cadet without telling anyone. People will only know he belongs to the police force when they see him proudly wearing his uniform. Baptism is a way of showing that we belong to Jesus and that we aren't ashamed of our faith in Him. To belong to Jesus is an incredible privilege. He is the greatest teacher, healer, leader and Saviour the world has ever seen.

Paul said, *'I am not ashamed of the gospel!'* (Romans 1:16) Jesus said, *'whoever acknowledges me before men, I will also acknowledge him before my Father in heaven. But whoever disowns me before men, I will disown him before my Father in heaven'* (Matthew 10:32–33).

When a girl is engaged, her fiancé gives her a ring, so that she can indicate to others that her life is linked with his.

What does she do with this outward sign of her inward attachment? Does she keep it secretly in its little box? Of course not! The ring is proudly worn on the hand for all to see. Let us be equally glad to confess that our lives belong to Jesus Christ. *'What are you waiting for? Get up, be baptised and wash your sins away'* (Acts 22:16).

3. OUR DEDICATION TO JESUS CHRIST

When a Roman soldier enlisted in the army he became committed to a life of loyalty and dedicated service to the Emperor. He showed his allegiance to the Emperor by making an oath called a 'sacramentum'. Jesus gave His disciples the two ordinances of baptism and the breaking of bread so that they could show their allegiance to Him, they are known as 'sacraments'.

A sacrament shows that a promise has been made. In a marriage service, the husband gives his wife a ring to show that he has promised to forsake all others and be married to his wife alone. When we decided to become a Christian we promised to follow Jesus. Baptism is a sign that shows that we have made this promise.

Baptism isn't a step to take lightly. It shows that we are dedicated to Jesus, and that means leaving behind the things that grieve Him and giving ourselves completely to Him. Separating ourselves from what we know is wrong and giving ourselves to Jesus go hand in hand. *'Do not offer the parts of your body to sin, as instruments of wickedness, but rather offer yourselves to God, as those who have been brought from death to life; and offer the parts of your body to him as instruments of righteousness'* (Romans 6:13). The step of baptism needs to be taken thoughtfully and seriously. We should regard it as an act of total dedication to our Lord and Master, an offering of our life to Him for all time. *'Therefore, I urge you, brothers, in view of God's mercy, to offer your bodies as living sacrifices, holy and pleasing to God – this is your spiritual act of worship'* (Romans 12:1).

It would be serious for a Roman soldier to go back on his oath and desert the ranks. It is very sad when marriage vows are broken. It is a tragedy when a Christian goes back to his old way of life. Let us determine, with God's help, never to turn back. Jesus said, *'No-one who puts his hand to the plough and looks back is fit for service in the kingdom of God'* (Luke 9:62). Satan will contest our dedication to Jesus Christ all the way by fierce temptations, bitter disappointments and even persecution.

In some countries today, Christians have to face imprisonment and even death following their baptism. It is really costly for them to take this step and yet they do so with courage and devotion to Jesus.

4. OUR IDENTIFICATION WITH JESUS CHRIST

This is the deeper meaning of baptism, which is brought out in the teaching of the apostles. The origin of Christian baptism is found in the Gospels, the practice of it in the book of Acts and the explanation of it in the Epistles. The main passage which deals with this aspect is Romans 6:3–14.

In baptism we are identified with Jesus Christ in His three great acts that secured our salvation – His death, burial and resurrection. Paul sums up the Christian message by linking these together; *'Christ died for our sins ... he was buried .. he was raised on the third day'* (1 Corinthians 15:3–4).

His identification with us

When Jesus first came he identified himself with sinners. He did this by coming as a man, being clothed with our humanity and then in two other ways:

(1) By His Baptism in the River Jordan. John baptised those who repented in response to his preaching. When Jesus asked John to baptise Him, John at first refused. This was because John knew that Jesus had no need of repentance. Jesus went down into the water in order to stand in the sinner's place. He identified Himself with them in their relation to God as sinners. His baptism in the River Jordan was also a picture of His death, and His coming up from the water, a portrayal of His resurrection.

(2) By His Baptism on The Cross. Jesus said *'I have a baptism to undergo, and how distressed I am until it is completed!'* (Luke 12:50). Jesus was referring to the time when He would be overwhelmed by mental agony, physical pain and spiritual anguish on the cross. He was immersed in suffering as He bore God's judgment for our sins. In His life and in His death, Jesus, who was sinless, took the place of those who were sinful.

Our identification with Him

When we became Christians, two things happened: our old way of life finished and a completely new way of life began. This is summed up in Romans 6: *'Count yourselves dead to sin but alive to God in Christ Jesus'* (Romans 6:11). The moment our lives were linked with Jesus, the two things that happened to Him, happened also to us. We died with Him to sin and its power over us, and we rose with Him to a new life. These great truths are clearly demonstrated in baptism by immersion.

INTO THE WATER
DEATH

As we go down into the water we are saying in effect, that just as Jesus died for our sin on the cross, so we too have died to sin in our lives. There has been a complete break with the past – a death – *'count yourselves dead to sin'* (Romans 6:11). The phrase 'dead to sin' may seem unfamiliar to us but its practical meaning is important and clear. If a person is so engrossed in reading the newspaper that all attempts to divert his attention fail, then we might say, 'He is dead to the world.' By this we mean that he is insensitive to, or not conscious of, our attempts to entice him away from the newspaper. We need to be so absorbed in our rich friendship with Jesus that the temptations of the enemy pass us by.

UNDER THE WATER
BURIAL

A dead person must be buried. Just as Jesus Christ was buried in the tomb, so when we are lowered beneath the water, our lives as sinners are regarded as put out of sight. The Bible teaches, *'we were therefore buried with him through baptism into death'* (Romans 6:4). Our baptism then becomes a kind of funeral, and the water a grave, by which a declaration is made to all that the sinner we once were has died and needs to be buried. Death followed by burial now prevents us from returning to our former way of life. This is why Paul asks the question, *'We died to sin; how can we live in it any longer?'* (Romans 6:2).

OUT OF THE WATER
RESURRECTION

'We were therefore buried with him through baptism into death in order that, just as Christ was raised from the dead through the glory of the Father, we too may live a new life. If we have been united with him like this in his death, we will certainly also be united with him in his resurrection' (Romans 6:4–5). Jesus Christ was raised from the dead by the power of God. We are lifted from the water to live a new and distinctive life, the life of a true Christian. Paul wrote, *'I have been crucified with Christ and I no longer live, but Christ lives in me. The life I live in the body, I live by faith in the Son of God, who loved me and gave himself for me'* (Galatians 2:20).

The life we live as Christians must express these two great truths, that we are dead to sin and alive to God. An illustration from nature will help us to see this more clearly. Some flowers close up at night when the darkness falls, but open out when morning breaks and the sun shines. They are dead to the dark and alive to the light, closed to one sphere but open to the other. In the Bible, darkness is often linked with evil, and light with purity. Jesus said, *'Men loved darkness instead of light because their deeds were evil'* (John 3:19), and *'I am the light of the world. Whoever follows me will never walk in darkness, but will have the light of life'* (John 8:12). Like the flowers, our lives must be closed to those things which we know are dark and evil, and wide open to the light and love of God, see Romans 6:11.

To live the new life we have been given is a continual challenge. Every day we will sense the downward pull of our sinful natures. But God has given us his Holy Spirit to come and live inside us, helping us to continue turning from our sinful nature and to live for Jesus. The Holy Spirit also helps to remind us that we are Christians. His constant work in our lives stops us relying just on the past experiences of conversion and baptism for assurance. With the help of the Spirit, we can battle sin and temptation. We need His help as without Him Satan is too strong for us.

Having been baptised we must not think that we have reached the end of the road; in reality it is only part of the beginning. *'So then, just as you received Christ Jesus as Lord, continue to live in him, rooted and built up in him, strengthened in the faith as you were taught, and overflowing with thankfulness'* (Colossians 2:6–7). Those who became Christians in the New Testament were nearly always baptised immediately, so their knowledge and experience of Jesus was only just beginning. In Acts 2 the new converts did not stand still after being baptised, they moved on to those things that would build up their faith. This brings us to the next step, which deals with our progress as Christians.

Those who became Christians in the New Testament were nearly always baptised immediately, so their knowledge and experience of Jesus was only just beginning.

Questions to answer

1. List three ways in which we can show others that we are Christians.

2. Write out two of the verses that indicate baptism should follow belief in Christ.

3. Write a note on the place of obedience in relation to baptism.

4. Why should the step of baptism be taken seriously?

5. What are we declaring in the following three actions in our baptism?

a Into the water

b Under the water

c Out of the water

To think over:

Is there any good reason why I should not obey the command of Christ to be baptised?

Step 6

CONTINUING WITH JESUS

'Those who accepted his message were baptised, and about three thousand were added to their number that day. They devoted themselves to the apostles' teaching and to the fellowship, to the breaking of bread and to prayer' (Acts 2:41–42). The apostles taught the new Christians the next steps in the Christian life. The converts immediately became involved in the worship and witness of the Christian church.

Jesus sent the disciples into the world to preach the gospel and to baptise those who would believe. He then added, *'teaching them to obey everything I have commanded you'* (Matthew 28:20). Preaching the Gospel, baptising the converts and teaching the commandments of Jesus sums up the work of the Christian church. The first section of this booklet dealt with believing the gospel, the second with being baptised, and the third deals with the continuing life of the Christian. Being baptised then is not an end in itself, but a part of the developing life of our Christian experience. Here are four vital things to which we need to devote ourselves:

THE APOSTLES' TEACHING

Jesus Christ spent three years teaching His disciples before sending them into the world to teach others. The things they taught the people by word of mouth are written down for us in the

New Testament. If we are to devote ourselves to the apostles' teaching it will be necessary for us to do three things:

a. Read the Bible regularly

Time needs to be set aside each day for the reading of God's Word. Only in this way can we feed ourselves and grow strong spiritually. The Bible is our food, and if we neglect to read it, our faith will wither and even die. Make sure you have some Bible reading notes to guide you. It will be necessary, not only to read the Bible quietly by ourselves, but also to read it regularly with others in home groups and church services, where the meaning of God's Word is explained. This is how we build up our faith and discover God's will for our lives. In the preface to the Gideon's Bibles you will find these words: *'It contains light to direct you, food to support you, comfort to cheer you and armour to protect you. It is the traveller's map, the pilgrim's staff, the pilot's compass, the soldier's sword and the Christian's charter.'*

b. Apply the Bible prayerfully

We must not read the Bible merely as an academic exercise, but think primarily of how we can prayerfully interpret its teaching and how we can apply God's instructions to our daily lives. Before reading it is good to pray, *'Open my eyes that I may see wonderful things in your law'* (Psalm 119:18). By ourselves we shall not understand all that we read, we need the help of the Holy Spirit. When we have taken in a part of God's Word, it is good to go back and pray over it asking the Holy Spirit to interpret it to us.

c. Obey the Bible continually

It is so easy to fail to put into practice the things we learn from the Bible. This we are told in God's Word is sin: *'Anyone, then, who knows the good he ought to do and doesn't do it, sins'* (James 4:17). *'Do not merely listen to the word, and so deceive yourselves. Do what it says'* (James 1:22). To obey God is often costly, but He will always provide the strength we need to do what He asks.

To devote ourselves to the apostles' teaching is to cling to the Word of God, especially when we are being tested. Paul said to Timothy, *'continue in what you have learned and have become convinced of'* (2 Timothy 3:14). Jesus said, *'if you hold to my teaching, you are really my disciples'* (John 8:31).

FELLOWSHIP

Christian fellowship refers to the close and intimate relationship people share both with Jesus Christ and with other believers. The early Christians thrived on this deep sense of friendship as they worshipped together, witnessed together, prayed together and enjoyed being together. They shared in each other's joys and sorrows. They helped and encouraged one another. In Acts

2:44–46 we get a clear picture of the common life they enjoyed. They were bound together by the invisible bond of Christ's love, which was the source of their unity and strength, especially in days of persecution. It has been said that blood ties are the strongest ties. This is particularly true amongst Christians who realise they have been purchased by the precious blood of Christ. There are two aspects of fellowship we need to develop:

a. Fellowship with Jesus

In 1 Corinthians 1:9 we read, *'God, who has called you into fellowship with his Son Jesus Christ our Lord, is faithful.'* God has called us to share in the life of His Son, which means we can continually experience His joy and peace and strength in our lives. This is something we need to develop, so that our fellowship with Him grows stronger and stronger. It is rewarding to discover that the closer we get to Jesus, the closer we want to get, and the deeper our friendship becomes, the deeper we want it to be. After many years on the Christian pathway, Paul's great longing was still *'I want to know Christ'* (Philippians 3:10).

b. Fellowship with others

John speaks not only of *'fellowship with the Father and with His Son, Jesus Christ'* (1 John 1:3), but refers also to having *'fellowship with one another'* (1 John 1:7). This arises out of and depends upon our fellowship with God. Jesus has not only drawn us close to Himself, but united us as Christians to each other. We are members of a large and wonderful family with Jesus as the Head. We belong not only to Christ, but also to one another. Just as the spokes of a bicycle wheel are joined to the hub at the centre and to the rim at the circumference, so each Christian is joined to Christ who is the centre of our fellowship, and joined also to every other believer in the wider circle of Christian fellowship. As individual Christians then, as spokes in the wheel, we must make sure that we retain continual contact with Jesus and close contact with Christians, in order to maintain spiritual vitality and the unity of the church. Trouble begins when the spoke comes adrift at either end.

No Christian was ever meant to go it alone. We need to spend time with Jesus and with others of like mind. 'Birds of a feather flock together' and as Christians we need to keep together or the pressures of the world and the opposition of Satan will weaken our faith. This means every Christian needs to belong to a place of worship where God's word is faithfully preached, and attend regularly the services that are arranged. *'Let us not give up meeting together, as some are in the habit of doing, but let us encourage one another – and all the more as you see the Day approaching'* (Hebrews 10:25). If we stay away from

Christian fellowship our love for the Lord Jesus will soon grow cold, just as a piece of coal taken out of a fire and placed on the hearth soon becomes cold and lifeless. To be in the company of keen Christians is like being in the centre of a fire. When we are together, with Jesus in the midst, He kindles a fire of love in our hearts which generates warm Christian fellowship.

It is a great privilege to belong to a group of Christians, but it carries with it the responsibility of doing all we can to contribute to the smooth running and spiritual wellbeing of the fellowship. Let us be careful not to divide and spoil the fellowship by unkind words or selfish actions. Satan loves to weaken the effectiveness of Christians by creating divisions among them.

BREAKING OF BREAD

To eat together has always been a sign of fellowship, especially in the East. But the term used here, 'breaking of bread', means something more than simply sharing an ordinary meal. It refers to the Lord's Supper or the communion service. Jesus took bread and wine, the two most common elements of an Eastern meal, and used them as a picture of His body and His blood. By breaking bread together, the disciples were doing what Jesus had asked them to do. He instituted and requested this before He died, in order that they might keep Him continually in their minds.

a. It was instituted by Jesus

The first three gospels clearly explain how the communion meal was arranged by Jesus, (Matthew 26:26–30; Mark 14:22–25; Luke 22:19–20 & 1 Corinthians 11:23–32). On the very night in which Jesus was betrayed, He was eating a meal with His disciples in the upper room. While they were eating, He took some bread, gave thanks, broke it and distributed it amongst the disciples saying, *'This is my body given for you; do this in remembrance of me'* (Luke 22:19). He also took a cup of wine, and after giving thanks passed it to His disciples saying, *'This cup is the new covenant in my blood, which is poured out for you'* (Luke 22:20). The disciples would not

Jesus has not only drawn us close to Himself, but united us as Christians to each other. We are members of a large and wonderful family with Jesus as the Head. We belong not only to Christ, but also to one another.

at that time have understood the full significance of what Jesus Christ had said and done, but He knew the painful truth. He had come to give His body and shed His life's blood for the sins of the world, and therefore He took the simple elements of bread and wine to portray these profound truths.

b. It was requested by Jesus

Jesus Christ asked His disciples to continue this symbolic act of remembrance of Himself. When He instituted the service, He said, *'Do this in remembrance of me.'* The words 'do this' are in the present continuous tense, which means keep on doing this until I come again. If we have obeyed the command of Jesus to be baptised, we must also respond to His request to break bread in memory of Him. These are the only two ordinances Jesus gave us.

He knew just how forgetful we would be and how prone to stray from Him, so He instituted this simple but powerful visual aid. It reminds us continually of the depth of His sacrificial love for each one of us, the great price He paid to set us free from our sin and self-centredness. Let us be at this important communion service as often as possible, or our hearts will grow cold, and we will forget the One who died to give us life.

PRAYERS

Those who believed and were baptised *'devoted themselves ... to prayer'* (Acts 2:42). The fourth activity in which the new converts continued steadfastly is described as *'the prayers'* (RSV). This indicates they had set times when they met together for united prayer. Private prayer is vital to the spiritual life of the individual, while public and corporate prayer is essential for the spiritual wellbeing of any fellowship. Prayer has been likened to breathing. Without it there cannot be life or growth.

a. Private prayer

The need to live a life of private prayer was taught by Jesus. *'When you pray, go into your room, close the door and pray to your Father, who is unseen. Then your Father who sees what is done in secret, will reward you'* (Matthew 6:6). The example of a life of private prayer was given by Jesus. Mark records in his Gospel that *'very early in the morning, while it was still dark, Jesus got up, left the house and went off to a solitary place, where he prayed'* (Mark 1:35). If Jesus found it necessary to pray, how much more should we?

Prayer is rather like using a telephone. It is our line of communication with God. We can dial right through at any time and for any reason. Just as a telephone has a part for listening and a part for speaking, so we need to look upon prayer as a conversation we enjoy with God, rather than a speech we make or a shopping list we present to God. God wants to speak to us. The main way that God has spoken to us is through the Bible. Reading the Bible helps us to build our relationship with God as we get to know Him better, and find out how He wants us to live. We can speak to God in prayer about things we have read in the Bible and we can ask Him to help us understand anything that we find difficult.

b. Public prayer

While it is important to have set times of prayer alone, it is also a great source of strength and blessing to pray with others. Too many neglect public prayer meetings and so deprive themselves and the church of blessing and progress.

Peter knew the power of prayer because we are told, *'many people had gathered and were praying'* (Acts 12:12), and as a result he was delivered from prison. Paul sought the prayers of the churches and often sent them prayer requests, e.g. *'Brothers, pray for us that the message of the Lord may spread rapidly and be honoured, just as it was with you. And pray that we may be delivered from wicked and evil men'* (2 Thessalonians 3:1–2). When the people of God pray, the preaching of His Word will prevail. We owe it to ourselves and we owe it to others to live a life of prayer.

It is important not only to become a Christian and to be baptised, but also to continue living the Christian life in fellowship with others and in a deepening relationship with Jesus. While in Antioch, Paul and Barnabas spoke to the converts and *'urged them to continue in the grace of God'* (Acts 13:43). They returned later strengthening the disciples and encouraging them to remain true to the faith. *'We must go through many hardships to enter the kingdom of God'* (Acts 14:22).

Questions to answer

1. How can you make sure you will progress as a Christian and not go back to your old way of life?

2. What place should the Bible have in our lives?

3. Why is Christian fellowship so necessary?

4. Why should Christians 'break bread' together?

5. Why is prayer so important for the Christian?

APPENDIX

PRACTICAL DETAILS FOR THOSE GETTING BAPTISED

1. Having read this booklet and the relevant passages in the Bible, you may want to obey the command of Jesus Christ to be baptised. If this is so, then your next step is to express your desire to your minister or a leader in your church, who will discuss the arrangements with you as well as explain anything you do not understand.

2. If the church to which you belong agrees to baptise you and you are still very young, it will be necessary to have your parents' permission. Should you have any difficulties at home, a Christian from your church will always call and speak with your parents.

3. Invite your family, relatives and friends to attend the service. It is an opportunity to show other people how much Jesus means to you. Someone else may become a Christian or be baptised as a result of your witness.

4. You may want to think carefully about where the baptism is to take place. Some people are baptised in church buildings, others in a river or the sea where many more may witness the event.

5. Do wear suitable clothing. The person conducting the service will advise you on this and explain how everything will take place. If you have not previously witnessed a baptismal service, it would be good to take the opportunity of attending one if possible.

6. Ask a close friend to sit with you to support you, and to hand you a towel as you leave the water.

FOR THOSE BAPTISING

1. Explain carefully to those you are baptising how you want them to stand and how you will hold them. Make clear all the practical details surrounding their entering and leaving the water. The more informed they are, the more relaxed they will be.

2. Make sure that a maximum amount of water is in the baptistry as this makes baptising so much easier.

3. It is helpful, though not necessary, to have two people doing the baptising. This gives a greater sense of security

to the person being baptised, as well as being easier in the event of baptising a heavy person, or several people being baptised during the service.

4. Do baptise slowly and gently as this gives greater dignity to this ordinance. Many baptise hurriedly and enthusiastically sending water in all directions. This tends to detract from the baptism, focusing people's minds on the 'splash' rather than the beautiful symbolism being portrayed. It also intimidates those thinking about baptism. This is a further reason for having two people baptising.

5. Always remember that a baptismal service will bring into the church many people who do not normally attend a place of worship. We want them to understand and value this important sacrament given to us by Jesus. Ensure that everything is done decently and in order.

6. It will be helpful if refreshments are available at the end of the service. This will create a relaxed atmosphere in which church members can meet and share with those attending for the first time.

7. In the following weeks, encourage the church to pray for those who have been baptised, as they will be special targets for Satan's temptations (see Matthew 3:16 – 4:11).

SOME FURTHER READINGS ON BAPTISM

IN THE GOSPELS

Baptism of John
Matthew 3:1–12, Mark 1:1–8, Luke 3:1–20,
John 1:15–28

Baptism of Jesus
Matthew 3:13–17, Mark 1:9–11, Luke 3:21–22, John 1:29–34

IN THE BOOK OF ACTS

Baptism of the Ethiopian:
Acts 8:26–40

Baptism of Saul:
Acts 9:18–19

Baptism of Cornelius and others:
Acts 10:47–48

Baptism of Lydia and her household:
Acts 16:14–15

Baptism of the jailer and his household:
Acts 16:25–34

Baptism of the Corinthians:
Acts 18:8

Baptism of John's disciples:
Acts 19:1–7

IN THE EPISTLES

Romans 6:1–11, 1 Corinthians 10:1–15, Galatians 3:27, Colossians 2:12–13, 1 Peter 3:18–22

Notes